10 Reasons why Startups outperform incumbents in the innovation game

Fernando Taliberti

Intentionally left blank

Copyright © 2012 Fernando Taliberti

Todos os direitos reservados.

ISBN: 9781973189008

Independently published

Intentionally left blank

Back in 1997, Harvard Professor Clayton Christensen published "The Innovator's Dilemma" and explained how hard it is for an established company to face disruptive innovation that threatens its business in the long term. Christensen explained many of the mechanisms that tend to keep incumbents inert while their competitors introduce innovations. The book was mainly dedicated to study the effects of 'disruptive' innovations on established companies.

We can discuss later what disruptive means, but in short, the term usually refers to something revolutionary for a whole industry and not just any radical innovation. However, any established company facing an innovation representing a radical new way of doing business will deal with the same challenges described by the author. The inertia of incumbents many times sets competitive advantages to market entrants, in many cases startups beginning from scratch.

Many of the forces that create those challenges get more obvious when a startup is compared to an incumbent. Let us have a look at 10 of them:

1—An early market may be very attractive for the startup and uninteresting for an incumbent

It is now widely known that Apple had access to some innovations, such as the mouse and the Graphic User Interface (GUI), developed at Xerox Palo Alto Research Center (PARC). These innovations were incorporated into the Mac and helped Apple change the computer industry, but were not invented by Steve Jobs' team. The PARC personnel presented them to the team from Apple that could make a better use of this technology.

The PARC was an ivory tower isolated from the Xerox headquarters and researched technologies that could change the company's industry. Documents and images becoming digital surely had to do with this change. In that sense having such a research center was the right thing to do to perpetuate the company's dominance, however, it was not enough. Developing a new business requires a lot more investment from a company than just in research. It requires the determination to enter a new market. Naturally, to take this decision, the new market is compared to the existing markets in which the company has businesses and should seem equally or more attractive.

Anyone who has watched the movie 'Pirates of the Silicon Valley' (1999) will remember the scene in which the company's brass watches a presentation from the PARC researchers and makes fun of the mouse, saying "you want Xerox to consider something called a mouse?". It wouldn't be a natural choice for Xerox to enter the personal computer business. A multi billion-dollar company would be expected to postpone the decision to enter any market that was incipient compared to the one they dominated as the potential revenue simply doesn't seem to compensate the risk of the investment. So established companies will focus on larger projects and markets and will easily ignore what starts really small and grows really fast.

2—The same absolute growth may mean a lot for a startup and be irrelevant for an incumbent

Tesla was founded in 2003 and took 3 years to release its first electric car. Since then it grows steadily, leading a new market that is still incipient compared to the internal combustion vehicles' market. Looking back at the company numbers in 2010, we see a company with 116 million dollars in revenues. An exciting number for a 7 years old company, but not so interesting for Volkswagen AG, which had revenues of 126 billion Euros (about 143 billion dollars) and grew 20% in comparison with 2009. A company this big with such a growth rate would hardly consider entering a market as small as Tesla's since the growth space there would be so small in absolute terms. Even if it did, sustaining investments in a new business for seven years, after which it is still not very significant to the eyes of the company's management, would require a lot of political alignment. The C level and the board would have to be very convinced of the importance of the new business for the future of the corporation, not to shut down the project. On the other end, for a Venture Capitalist the growth of a company such as Tesla is enough to make it an attractive investment and have investors lining up for each investment round.

Now take Tesla's announced 2014 revenue of 3.2 billion dollars. It grew 60% year over year (1.2 billion), whilst Volkswagen Group now has revenues around 200 billion Euros, but now with growth rates around 2%. Tesla's growth in absolute terms would now make a difference to Volkswagen's growth. But as Christensen puts it, "it is too late to plant a tree when you need the shadow".

3—Any positive margin is an improvement

Amazon's history is probably the best example for this matter. Ever since it was a startup, Amazon seeks to offer the best prices to its customers, usually with very little gross margins. Exploring a new digital channel exclusively, Amazon believed it could scale quickly and make money with the increase of the sales volume. With this strategy, the company has grown insanely. It started with books, but since it was a business with virtually no margin, adding new categories was equally, or more attractive.

For an established retailer however, dropping down margins to compete with Amazon was much harder, since they had a history of profitability and investors expectations to meet.

This is how the newcomer Amazon has threatened incumbents such as Walmart and Barnes & Noble, gaining unprecedented space in the market by exploring the online channel.

4—They don't have biased incentive models

Growth, Revenues, Margin... This kind of performance indicator is usually ingrained in the established companies' metrics and comprises the KPI's for variable pay of most employees, from the junior business analyst to the CEO. Other types of financial incentive models, such as sales commissions, are even stronger in forging inertia. Imagine a company that sells software in a licensing model. Take Siebel (the CRM company acquired by Oracle). The salespeople were used to selling licenses for thousands of dollars per user and being awarded generous commissions. Now imagine a competitor such as Salesforce.com enters the market with a subscription-based model, very attractive to the clients. How hard would it be for Siebel to introduce a new model to face Salesforce.com where the salesperson would have to sell a cheaper product and earn less commission? And it is not only the salespeople incentives that are at stake in such a case. Changing the revenue model, or even introducing a new one, would impact the KPI's of many people between a salesperson and the CEO making it a very tough medicine for the company to swallow.

The timeframe is another problem regarding incentive models. Usually companies evaluate and reward their employees yearly. That means that yearly targets must be established for everyone, including people involved in innovation projects. This kind of project, however, should aim high level, long-term targets and should be very open to change course if necessary. KPI's for variable pay, on the other hand, must be short-term, specific, measurable and stable. That usually means the team's targets quickly loose alignment with the project, but since it is hard to change them, the team keeps seeking them, biased toward wrong objectives.

5—They have no processes that need to be changed

Changing incentive models maybe hard enough, but an established company's processes are usually brewed for many years. They become supported by systems that optimize and automate parts of them, many hours of training were invested to make them work and people get attached to them. When an innovation requires a radical change of these processes it is usually much harder for an established company to embrace it than for a startup which usually has no process at all.

When Netflix started, it sent DVDs to customers' houses by mail (and it still does, believe me). The whole process was very efficient and didn't need all the real estate Blockbuster had to rent it's DVDs. Sounds simple, so why didn't Blockbuster introduce the new process in parallel? Well, it couldn't do it exactly the same way as Netflix. It would probably try to optimize its DVD inventory mixing both models and would have to offer both of them to the same customers. That means it couldn't only introduce a new process. It would have to change its current processes, and this is much harder.

6—They have no business model to threaten

Sometimes it is not only about financial models and indicators and processes. The whole company's business model may be very hard to change. Take Kodak. The cycle of photography was complex and Kodak had businesses built all over it, from film supply to developing, including the camera's supply, of course. The digital photography has made all this cycle obsolete, together with Kodak's business model. Then it became not only a matter of entering a new market, which Kodak was already doing, but shifting the whole business model of a huge company. Sounds like steering a transatlantic, and it is.

7—They are more flexible in creating the necessary core competences

Google was already a powerhouse when Facebook was founded. It had very strong competences in algorithms and machine learning. Social, however, was never part of Google's core competences. Curiously, in the same year that Facebook was founded, a social network was born inside Google as a result of the company's policy that lets employees work in their side projects: Orkut. But Orkut never seemed to be recognized as an official Google Product until it was shut down in 2014, three years later than Google+ was launched.

In the mean time Facebook grew, first focused in universities, then as a more general social network, to an astonishing success Google never achieved with neither its social products.

As a new chapter in the same novel, Waze surged in Israel and has gained the world combining social features with a lot of algorithms in order to deliver the best routes for any commuter that wanted to escape traffic. Google Maps had been in the market for many years and even offered some traffic information. But what Waze could do, powered by the information shared socially by all its users, Google Maps couldn't. In 2013, Google acquired Waze, a company with a product that wouldn't be created inside the company, due to the lack of social as one of its core competences.

It is interesting to note that customers don't easily adopt products that are not based on the company's core competences. Any Google product based on social features seems ill-fated compared to startup's products connected to Facebook as Google Buzz and Google Wave have shown.

8—They need to be less careful about their MVPs

Apple is known by the impeccable design of its products that have revolutionized industries. But it was once a startup and it had an MVP (Minimum Viable Product, the concept introduced by Eric Ries in the book "The Lean Startup"). This is what the Apple I looked like back in 1976.

The Apple I—Source: Wikipedia

It doesn't look like a product of the company as we know today. And it certainly wouldn't look like an IBM product if the Big Blue had decided to enter the Personal Computer market in the same date. But all the care an established company usually puts in the launch of a new product means it takes longer and bears a lot more costs to reach the market than a startup does. So it collects market feedback and iterates launching better products much later. For the enthusiasts of *The Lean Startup*, it is clear that the startup in this case will run leaner and achieve success sooner.

9—They have a focused and free founding team

The founders of a startup have no bias or norm to conform to when thinking their product from scratch. In contrast, in many cases a team creating something new in a corporation will have to conform to established norms. Could you imagine a team creating a messenger app inside Facebook and not using Facebook ID to sign in? The same is difficult to imagine inside Google. If this team had some requisite that Facebook ID wouldn't meet, they'd have to spend a lot of time specifying that to another team and wait for its delivery (as if it was that simple).

Now take the WhatsApp founding team. They didn't restrain the usage of their app by being in a network, such as Facebook with "merely" hundreds of millions of users. They simply used the phone number as ID to maximize the potential size of their network. And so, they stayed focused on building the simplest messaging app they could think of.

10—Legacy

Be it a licensed CRM, an existing messaging app or a high end product that shouldn't be disrupted, established companies have legacies. Innovators inside of them must dodge this legacy or face the wrath of the people who may feel their products or business are being threatened.

If instead of Salesforce.com, Oracle/Siebel was to launch a SaaS CRM product, it would feel awkward for everybody in the established business, let alone their clients that paid thousands for a license of Siebel. If Facebook was to launch a messaging app that used the phone number as ID, creating no synergies with their network, how much questioning would there be inside the company? If IBM was to launch a personal computer that looked like the Apple I, it wouldn't comply to their standards and, probably, would not hit the streets.

All the weight the incumbent carries from their existing products and businesses may be considered legacy and may comprise obstacles for internal innovations that could challenge them.

Intentionally left blank

Intentionally left blank

Startups looking to outperform established companies may look for the conflicts of interest that lie within these ten factors. However, since the publishing of "The Innovator's Dilemma", many established companies have been aware of it and have managed to deal with and circumvent them. Startups should be aware of that too.

Still, there's a lot of beauty in the cycle of a company being born from an innovation and creating a lot of stability around it until it is threatened by another innovation from the outside. That creates a lot of space for the surging of new Googles and Facebooks from time to time and I bet this cycle will never stop, no matter how good incumbents get in reinventing themselves.

About the Author

Fernando Taliberti is a Industrial Engineer from Federal University of Rio de Janeiro and a Master's degree in e-Business and Technologies for Management by Politecnico di Torino. He has more than 15 years of experience working as a consulting executive in Strategy, Management and Technology projects, as well as having led TOTVS Ventures (TOTVS Startups investment arm) and has been a director of M & A (Mergers and Acquisitions) of TOTVS. He is currently Co-Founder of Onyo, a Startup of Mobile Order Ahead that gives consumers the ability to place their order in restaurants in mobile phone markets, combining their vision of processes, management, technology and strategy in their own company.

https://www.linkedin.com/in/taliberti/

www.ingramcontent.com/pod-product-compliance
Lightning Source LLC
Chambersburg PA
CBHW031522210526
45464CB00007B/3007